The Day of the Disaster

THE BOMBING OF PEARL HARBOR

Written By: Sue L. Hamilton

NOTE: The following is a fictional account based on factual data.

Published by Abdo & Daughters, 6537 Cecilia Circle, Edina, Minnesota 55435.

Library bound edition distributed by Rockbottom Books, Pentagon Tower, P.O. Box 36036, Minneapolis, Minnesota 55435.

Copyright © 1991 by Abdo Consulting Group, Inc., Pentagon Tower, P.O. Box 36036, Minneapolis, Minnesota 55435. International copyrights reserved in all countries. No part of this book may be reproduced in any form without written permission from the publisher. Printed in the United States.

Library of Congress Number: 91-073041   ISBN: 1-56239-059-7

Cover Photo by: UPI Bettmann
Inside Photos by: UPI Bettmann

Edited by: John Hamilton

SUNDAY, DECEMBER 7, 1941
ISLAND OF OAHU, HAWAII

This Sunday dawned much as any other in the beautiful blue Pacific. The sun rose through partly cloudy skies sending sparkling rays of light dancing across the ocean. The bright morning light reflected off seven huge United States battleships tied up in a neat row by Ford Island, a tiny piece of land in the middle of Pearl Harbor.

The strategically located Island of Oahu harbored most of the United States Pacific Fleet. On this December day, only the two aircraft carriers, *Enterprise* and *Lexington*, were out to sea. All other ships and planes remained in port.

At 7:55 a.m., Army and Naval officers and troops were just beginning their usual Sunday morning routines — some showering, others getting dressed, eating breakfast — when the sound of plane engines reached their ears.

Nothing unusual. A typical morning as a group of pilots flew their daily reconnaissance mission. However, the next sounds were different — the high-pitched whistles of incoming bombs!

The blasts rocked Pearl Harbor. Japanese Zeros and Torpedo planes were everywhere! Flying high, diving low. Guns blasting, bombs dropping. With amazing accuracy, it took only minutes for the skilled pilots of Japan's Imperial Fleet to turn the harbor into a fiery disaster of mangled steel and thick black smoke.

Taken completely by surprise, the stunned members of the Pacific Fleet quickly realized they were faced with a full scale . . .

. . . Attack!

The Pacific fleet after the Japanese attack on Pearl Harbor.

FORWARD - THE ROAD TO WAR

JAPAN 1928 — Growth and Despair

Japan is a nation in trouble. Its population is growing by the millions. With its mountainous terrain, less than a quarter of its land can be farmed. The country of 145,809 sq. miles (slightly smaller than Montana) has little mineral resources such as iron or oil. Japan is outgrowing itself.

JAPAN 1930 — Military Take-Over

The free-speaking Democratic ideas of the early 1920s are gone. Powerful military officers seek control of the nation. Comparing themselves to the *samurai* warriors of the past, they systematically begin to take over the government, arresting and imprisoning those who try to stop them.

JAPAN 1931 — Invasion of China

Against the wishes of Emperor Hirohito, ruler of Japan, the Japanese army sends troops across the Sea of Japan into the country of Manchuria, in northeast China. Here, Japan already owns a railroad, iron works, coal mines, and other businesses. Acting without consent of the Japanese government, military forces invade Mukden, the capital of Manchuria. The city is brought under Japan's rule. This is the beginning of Japanese expansion.

JAPAN 1938 — Naval Build-Up
The voices of those determined to expand Japan's borders become louder and more aggressive. Military build-up continues. Through the 1930s the Japanese navy grows with well-armed warships, huge aircraft carriers, and some of the world's best planes: the Mitsubishi A6M2 Zero fighters, Nakajima B5N2 'Kate' torpedo bombers and Aichi D3A2 'Val' dive-bombers. Their soldiers are well-trained and disciplined. They prepare for . . .

WAR!

Germany's Third Reich marches through the streets of Munich during World War II.

SEPTEMBER 1939
World War II begins with Germany's invasion of Poland.

APRIL 1940
United States Army and Naval troops and ships, including eight Naval destroyers and two aircraft carriers, are moved from their mooring in San Diego, California to a central base in the Pacific: Pearl Harbor, Hawaii.

JUNE 1940
Italy enters the war, joining forces with Germany. German forces march into Paris, taking control of Northern France.

AUGUST 1940
The Battle of Britain begins with the German Air Force flying daily bombing raids over London and other British cities.

With allied countries needing troops at home to protect against invading German and Italian forces, countries such as the Philippines (controlled by the U.S.), Malaya (Britain) Indochina (France) and the East Indies (the Netherlands) are left virtually unprotected. These defenseless territories, rich in oil, coal, iron and other raw materials, are just what Japan needs.

SEPTEMBER 1940
Japan takes over northern Indochina. The United States, following its "Isolationist," or non-interference, policy, does little more than insist that Japan leave. Japan ignores the U.S. demand.

Germany and Italy, impressed with Japan's military success, invite Japan to sign the Tripartite or Axis Pact on September 27, 1940. The three countries agree to come to one another's help if attacked by "a power not already engaged in war." In other words, the United States.

JANUARY 1941
As the months pass, the United States finds it more and more difficult to stay out of the war. Although President Franklin D. Roosevelt is reelected in 1940 while promising to keep peace

for the United States, he is not blind to what is happening in Europe and China. He continues building up the U.S. military, calling it the "arsenal of democracy."

JULY 1941

Japan becomes even more aggressive. On July 26, 1941, they move farther into southern Indochina. This time the U.S. takes action, freezing all Japanese cash and goods in the U.S. and cutting off all oil supplies to Japan. This brings the Japanese army and naval commands into agreement: extreme measures are now needed.

SEPTEMBER - OCTOBER 1941

Repeated attempts are made at peace. However, the U.S demands the Japanese quit the Tripartite Pact with Germany and Italy, withdraw from China and Southeast Asia, and furnish the U.S. with "open-door" or unlimited trade rights in China. The Japanese refuse. Japan finalizes plans to wage war on the Americans, the British, and the Dutch.

United States President Franklin Delano Roosevelt prepares to declare war on Japan.

NOVEMBER 20, 1941
Prime Minister Hideki Tojo sends a counter offer to President Roosevelt offering to withdraw from Indochina if the U.S. will leave the Philippines, cut off aid to southern China, and free Japanese assets in the U.S. — terms unacceptable to the U.S.

NOVEMBER 26, 1941
A plan, developed by Japanese Commander-in-Chief of the Combined Fleet, Admiral Yamamoto Isoroku, is put into action. Six aircraft carriers, two battleships, two heavy cruisers and 11 destroyers set sail. The target: the United States Pacific Fleet, Pearl Harbor, Hawaii. The attack date: December 7, 1941.

ATTACK!

As seen through the eyes of Lt. Commander Fuchida, head of the Japanese strike force . . .

0600 PACIFIC TIME

As the first wave of attack, we are boarding our aircraft. We are prepared. The planes are ready. Only the weather can stop our planes. The faintest rays of morning light shine across the black ocean as we begin our takeoff. I am confident. Our mission will be a success!

0700 PACIFIC TIME

Lt. Commander Shimazaki will be leading the second wave. They should be taking off from the carrier *Zuikaku* about now.

0730 PACIFIC TIME

Following behind me, our strike force flies in perfect formation. We have been in the air for 1½ hours. We have picked up the sounds of Hawaii: a radio station's signal will lead us right to Honolulu . . . Adjusting flight 5° to port, we lead the other 383 planes on towards destiny.

0750 PACIFIC TIME

The cloud cover has cleared! I see it — Pearl Harbor. Just as our reports noted — all the battleships are in port. Sadly, the aircraft carriers have not returned.

There are no enemy planes here. It is strangely quiet. Too good to be true? No! We have succeeded in our plan. They are unaware of our presence. I must radio Nagumo aboard the *Akagi* with the signal:

Tora! Tora! Tora!*

*"Tiger! Tiger! Tiger!" A prearranged signal, alerting the vice admiral aboard the flagship carrier that the Japanese planes had advanced to Pearl Harbor undetected. Victory was certain.

INVASION!

As reported by an officer aboard the battleship, *U.S.S Nevada*

0730 PACIFIC TIME

Sunday morning. Skies — partly cloudy. Weather — Warm. Another day in paradise. All the battleships — *California, Maryland, Oklahoma, Tennessee, West Virginia,* and *Arizona* — are quietly moored south of me here at Ford Island in Pearl Harbor. Only the *Pennsylvania* is missing from "Battleship Row" — dry docked on shore for repairs.

I've just finished breakfast. Many men have gotten up early to get that extra ration of a half-pint of milk. Quite a treat for those of us used to powdered everything.

It's been so quiet here. This waiting has to be worse than really seeing some action. Day after day, drill after drill. It's beautiful here in Hawaii, but I'd rather be home with my family.

0750 PACIFIC TIME
The band has moved on deck. Only ten minutes before we'll raise our colors. The flag corp is walking to their position on the fore deck.

0755 PACIFIC TIME
Myself and the other officers stand at attention, saluting as the band begins to play the *Star Spangled Banner*. Some darn fools, probably from one of the aircraft carriers *Lexington* or *Enterprise*, just flew over about 100 feet off the deck. I heard someone mutter something about reporting them for safety violations . . .

0756 PACIFIC TIME
Wait! What's going on here? Oh my gosh, those are Jap planes — 'Kate' torpedo bombers and Zero fighters!

The band is still playing . . . faster and faster! A 'Kate' just dropped a torpedo! Like fools, we wait for the song to end. As the last note rings out, everybody on deck turns and runs! The 'Kate' swerves off, it's rear gunner blasting a path of deadly bullets on our deck. Officers, sailors, and band members clutching their instruments dive for cover. Alert! Sound te alert! Battle stations! Battle stations!

All sense of time is lost . . .

Everywhere I look, the sky is filled with Jap planes. We've already taken a couple of hits. They're flying so low, I can see the Japanese pilots in their 'Kates.' There faces filled with determined grins. Above their helmets and goggles, white scarves with a red circle*.

These are well-trained fighter pilots and we're like sitting ducks out here. The battleships lined up two-by-two in a neat little row . . . unprepared, unprotected and unable to escape. How could this happen? Why wasn't there a warning?

We've been hit! A torpedo in the port bow. The blast knocked me right off my feet. Can anything be as awful as the screaming whistle of an incoming bomb? I thought the harbor, only 40 ft. deep, was too shallow to allow for the dropping of torpedoes, but the Jap planes aren't having any problem! Judging from the looks of the harbor, every one of our battleships has already taken hits.

Hachimaki — A headband originally worn by medieval samurai when going into battle. Believed to bring good luck, it usually had a religious phrase inked around the traditional Japanese red rising sun.

The guns! Sombody has to get to the guns! Fire extinguishers! There's smoke everywhere. Fires . . . men on fire, equipment on fire, even the water surrounding us is ablaze! The captain has already ordered damage control. He's going to try to get us out of here.

It's hard to see; hard to think. There's so much noise and confusion. The yelling, the screams of agony. Medic! Over here! Can it be only a few moments ago we were eating breakfast? The deck is littered with dead, dying, and injured. Blood and oil mix to form a gruesome coating on deck. Hard to walk on. Is this happening?

I'm almost to the guns. There are men up there now. They're an open target for the Zeros! The smoke is choking me. I can't see clearly. I can't breathe.

Look out! Incoming!

The rising whine of the dive-bomber reaches my ears only seconds before the detonation. As though in slow motion, I dive for cover. I'm hit! My chest. The pain . . . I can't breathe. We're listing to one side . . . Are we going to have to abandon ship? Wait, the engines are moving. We're pulling out.

I'm losing blood fast. It's rolling down the deck. I can't get up. Medic! Help! Can anyone hear me? I'm losing consciousness . . . I . . . can't . . . breathe . . .

NOTE: Many men lost their lives aboard the battleships in Pearl Harbor. Hoping to make a run for open sea, the *Nevada* picked up steam and chugged away from its mooring at Ford Island. Japanese dive-bombers pursued it and further damaged the crippled battleship. Realizing that if the ship went down it would block the entire south entrance, she was beached away from the center of attack.

Japanese dive bombers destroyed many battleships in Pearl Harbor (above). The U.S.S. Phoenix *tries desperately to escape the bombardment.*

ATTACK!

As seen by an Army pilot at Wheeler Field — a United States Army Air Force fighter base in Oahu . . .

0800 — on . . .
We're under attack! The barracks just went up in smoke! It's the Japanese! Zeros everywhere. Lines of men headed for breakfast — they just stood there staring at the sky, unable to move. Even after the planes opened fire, they froze until they crumpled to the ground hurt or lifeless. Can this really be happening?

I've got to get to my plane. I can't believe that General Short ordered them parked wing-tip to wing-tip. They're all in nice lines. I know it was to prevent ground sabotage, but now one bomb from the air will take out a dozen or more!

The sky is filled with Jap planes. How could this happen? Wasn't there any warning? There must be hundreds of them!

Oh my gosh . . . the airfield is a mess! Already several planes have been hit! Fires . . . fire, smoke, men down!

Other pilots have gotten here before me. I watch as one tries to take off. Wait! He's on fire! BLAST! A huge fireball fills the sky. The explosion rocks the area as the burning wreck careens into another group of planes. The pilot . . . gone in an instant. His body shattered and scattered with his plane.

Incoming!

The stacatto blasts of machine-guns pepper across the airfield, while bombs drop like rain with each enemy air pass. There's no protection. We can't get a plane up in this. Even those that aren't yet on fire, the heat from the others is so intense, we can't get near them. Thick oily smoke blazes upwards, blinding and choking.

Incoming! No! Wait! It's one of ours! Stop shooting! It's the B-17s from the states!* They're trying to land! Stop firing!

Shrapnel, debris, parts of planes, and . . . my God . . . parts of men lie scattered on the air strip. We can't get the planes up, but even from here I can see the smoke rising above Pearl. The battleships were lined up, just like us here.

*Additional forces, 12 Army Air Corp. B-17 Flying Fortress bombers were expected on the morning of December 7, 1941. Ironically, the Japanese aircraft detected by radar, were dismissed as these B-17s. The American pilots flew right into the midst of the air attack. Out of gas and unprepared for battle, the planes were defenseless. Sadly, their biggest loss was at the hands of other U.S. ground forces, who mistakenly shot the B-17s as they tried to land.

We're under attack and powerless to help ourselves! Like flies on flypaper . . . we're stuck here just waiting to be squashed!

In the harbor, the U.S. Destroyer Shaw, goes up in flames, one of the first targets hit by the incoming Japanese fighter bombers.

RESCUE

As described by a Hawaiian civilian . . .

10:00 A.M.
The bombing has stopped. The Japanese planes are gone. Our harbor is a burning mess of smoke, destruction and death. All of the battleships are either capsized, heavily damaged, or sunk. The destruction is unbelievable.

I watched until the smoke was so thick, I couldn't see anything. I saw men diving into the water and trying to swim away only o come up in the center of an oily fire on the water. Burning, screaming, they dove back under . . . or died amidst the flames and smoke.

Myself and several other civilians have been asked to help with the men in the water. We'll do what we can.

11:45 A.M.
The sun is warm and clear. With each passing minute more smoke clears to show the complete devastation of America's Pacific Fleet. It's hard to believe that all this happened only this morning.

3:00 P.M.
The beautiful blue water is stained with ugly streaks of black oil and red blood, I swam out and brought in about 100 sailors. Some injured, several unconscious, and many dead. It's hard to tell who is dead and who's not. We drag them on shore and military personnel immediately get them up into ambulances and transport them to hospitals . . . or makeshift morgues.

I helped one man who had lost his hand by the wrist and was clutching some wreckage with his other arm. He looked at me and asked, "What happened?" I explained that the Japanese had attacked. He said, "Oh," and passed out.

6:00 P.M.
Bodies are still floating out in the water. I'm exhausted, but we'll work until it's dark. It'll take days to find all the men . . . if they can be found. The fires are still burning. I heard that when the *Arizona* went down, she broke the water main. Little water is reaching inland. The air bases are also on fire.

The bitter smell of burning oil still fills the air. I can smell it, taste it, feel it on my skin. This is the smell of war. The smell of disaster.

POSTSCRIPT —
"A DATE WHICH WILL LIVE IN INFAMY"

On December 6-7th, 1941, the U.S. military in Washington, D.C. had decoded a Japanese transmission to their Embassy clearly indicating an attack on Pearl Harbor was imminent. Through a series of bungled communications, neither Admiral Husband E. Kimmel, Commander-in-Chief of the U.S. Pacific Fleet, nor Lt. General Walter C. Short, Commander-in-Chief of the Army, were notified of the impending attack . . . until after it had begun. Then, General Short received a telegram: "The Japanese are presenting at 1:00 p.m. Eastern Standard Time what amounts to an ultimatum. Just what significance the hour set may have, we do not know. Be alert accordingly. George C. Marshall, Chief of Staff." 1:00 p.m. was, of course, 8:00 a.m. Pacific Time. Everyone on Oahu already knew what "significance" the hour meant.

The Japanese attack on Pearl Harbor crippled the United States Pacific Fleet:

- 2,330 servicemen killed; 1,145 wounded; 100 civilian casualties
- Eight battleships severely damaged or sunk:

  Arizona - A bomb plunged through several decks to go off in the forward magazine. The ship exploded and sank, trapping and killing more than a thousand crewmen.

  California - Received two torpedo hits. Despite her crews' efforts, she eventually sank.

  Maryland - High-level 'Kates' accurately bombed and crippled the ship.

  Nevada - A torpedo blasted a huge hole in its port bow. A short run for open sea was aborted. Crippled and on fire, it was beached inside the confines of the harbor.

  Oklahoma - Hit by torpedo fire, it capsized and sank to the harbor bottom. Only her keel remained above water.

Pennsylvania - Dry-docked for repairs, it received only one direct hit from the second wave of Japanese bombers.

Tennessee - Protected by the *Oklahoma* and *West Virginia*, it was not hit by torpedoes. However, an armour-piercing bomb blasted through five inches of armour in a turret and went off inside the ship. Fires broke out from burning debris thrown on it from the *Arizona*.

West Virginia - Six torpedos smashed into the ship. On fire, it sank to the bottom of the harbor.

- Minelayer *Oglala* and destroyers *Downes*, *Shaw* and *Cassin:* sunk or crippled.

- Nine other ships: sunk or crippled.

- 140 aircraft destroyed; 80 more damaged.

For all this destruction, the Japanese lost less than 100 military personnel, nine fighter planes, five torpedo-bombers, 15 dive-bombers, and five midget submarines (of which only one reached the harbor and that was sunk with depth charges from the destroyer *Monaghan* before it could do any damage.)

A fiery mass of steel, the U.S.S. West Virginia, *sinks to the bottom of Pearl Harbor.*

Although Japan wrecked great destruction on the Pacific Fleet, the aircraft carriers escaped, as did the dockyard installation and oil-storage facilities on Oahu. Of the eight battleships, only the *Arizona* and *Oklahoma* were forever lost in their watery graves. The others were righted and repaired (although it took many months for them all to be seaworthy again.)

In what is believed to have been one of the most costly Japanese tactical errors, General Nagumo chose not to send another wave of attacks back to finish off the Pacific Fleet. He believed that this was only the beginning of the war, and it was his duty to return the Imperial Fleet to Japan. This decision may well have cost Japan the war.

The effect of the Pearl Harbor attack was to bring together the American people. Those who formerly fought to stay out of war willingly and enthusiastically joined the military services. Suddenly, Japan was faced with a formidable enemy. As Vice-Admiral Yamamoto (the man who developed the Pearl Harbor plan of attack) said, "I fear all we have done is to awaken a sleeping giant and fill him with a terrible resolve."

The United States declared war on Japan on Monday, December 8, 1941. Three days later, Germany and Italy, standing up to their part of the Tripartite Agreement, declared war on the United States. America had entered World War II.

Little did Japan realize the real tragedy they would face some four years later with the fire bombing of Tokyo and the atomic horror of Hiroshima and Nagasaki. However, in December of 1941, the Empire of the Rising Sun was victorious. Heroes all, the Imperial Fleet steamed home to a welcoming celebration.

As for the United States, the country entered the war battered and embarrassed, but all the more determined to fight back. As President Roosevelt described it in his speech the following day to Congress, "December 7, 1941 — a date that will live in infamy." As we still remember: Pearl Harbor — America's day of disaster.